Beyond

The

Two party

Trap

The

Rise and Potential of America's

Third Parties

Gray Messer

DISCLAIMER

This book is an educational resource presenting the author's views on third-party politics in the United States. While the information is accurate and complete, the author does not guarantee its correctness or reliability. You should not rely on the book as legal, financial, or political advice. The author's views do not necessarily reflect the views of any organizations, platforms, or individuals mentioned in the book.

Table Of Contents

Introduction

Overview of the Current Political Landscape

The American political setting in 2024 will be characterized by upheaval and disappointment, with citizens disillusioned with both the Democratic and Republican parties. This unhappiness stems from perceived corruption, an incompetent government, and a failure to address the American people's most pressing needs.

Deep polarization in American culture has resulted in a political impasse in which compromise is unusual and legislative progress is frequently stalled by partisan gridlock. As economic inequality widens, the economy remains a key issue for many voters, resulting in stagnant salaries and increased living costs, particularly in housing and healthcare. Many Americans feel left behind by a system that appears to benefit the wealthy and well-connected.

The discussion over how to address these challenges, whether through a single-payer system, a public option, or market-based reforms, has been heated, with neither major party proposing a solution that will satisfy the majority of voters. Climate change is another issue in which many Americans believe the main parties have failed to take enough action.

Despite rising public awareness and concern about the effects of climate change, efforts to achieve comprehensive climate legislation have been continually thwarted by party bickering and the influence of big fossil industry lobbyists. Foreign policy is also a source of frustration, with many Americans skeptical of future military operations following the lengthy wars in Iraq and Afghanistan. The emergence of China as a global power, continued tensions with Russia, and the threat of international terrorism all pose complicated concerns that many believe the current political leadership is failing to address appropriately.

Another major concern is the influence of money in politics. The Supreme Court's decision in Citizens United v. FEC allowed corporations and unions to spend unlimited amounts of money on political campaigns, resulting in an explosion of campaign spending and increasing the power of wealthy donors and special interests. In this context, third-party candidates and independent movements have a unique opportunity to appeal to voters dissatisfied with the status quo and looking for solutions to the country's most serious issues.

However, they confront obstacles such as strict ballot access regulations, limited media coverage, and the belief that voting for a third-party candidate is a waste of time. However, the traditional two-party system is no longer enough for addressing complicated concerns. The advent of social media and digital platforms has opened up new opportunities for third-party candidates to connect with voters and gain grassroots support. As the electoral landscape shifts, a big third-party breakthrough remains a viable option.

Purpose Of The Book

This book analyzes the possibility of third-party politics in the United States, especially in the current political atmosphere. As frustration with the two major parties grows, there is a greater need for alternatives that can provide new answers and break the cycle of political deadlock.

The book offers a thorough assessment of the obstacles and opportunities that third-party candidates face, analyzing historical successes and failures to draw lessons for the future. It also offers a thorough examination of the contemporary political scene, including important problems fueling voter dissatisfaction such as economic inequality, healthcare, climate change, and the role of money in politics. The book provides practical advice and techniques for third-party candidates and their supporters, such as how to build a long-term political movement, engage and retain voters, and craft sustainable policy views that address the electorate's needs and concerns. It also calls into question the notion that voting for a third-party candidate is a waste of time, as many voters are hesitant to back a candidate they believe has no actual prospect of victory.

By emphasizing the impact that third-party politicians can have even if they do not win elections, the book hopes to reframe the narrative and urge more voters to consider third-party alternatives. The book also explores the prospects for electoral reform to level the playing field for third-party candidates, including ranked-choice voting, proportional representation, and other electoral systems that could result in a more equitable and representative democratic process. The book's goal is to inspire hope and action among people who believe in a better, more inclusive democracy by studying the possibility for third-party politics to provide a viable alternative to the current system.

CHAPTER 1

Historical Context

A Brief History of Third Parties in the U.S.

Third parties have played a significant role in American political history, often serving as catalysts for change and innovation. Despite the United States predominantly being a two-party system, various third parties have emerged over the years to challenge the dominance of the

Democratic and Republican parties. These parties have introduced new ideas, influenced major party platforms, and occasionally achieved significant electoral success.

One of the earliest third parties was the Anti-Masonic Party, founded in 1828, which was notable for being the first political party in the United States to hold a national convention to nominate its presidential candidate. Although it did not win the presidency, the party managed to elect a number of its members to Congress and state legislatures.

The Free Soil Party, founded in 1848, primarily focused on opposing the expansion of slavery into the western territories. While it did not win any presidential elections, the party managed to elect several members to Congress. The Free Soil Party eventually merged with the newly formed Republican Party in the 1850s, contributing to the latter's anti-slavery platform and setting the stage for the Republican Party's rise to prominence.

The Populist Party, also known as the People's Party, was another influential third party of the 19th century. Established in 1891, the party sought to represent the interests of farmers and laborers against the economic power of railroads, banks, and corporate monopolies. The party's platform included proposals for the direct election of senators, a progressive income tax, and government control of the railroads. The 1892 presidential election candidate, James B. Weaver, won over a million votes and carried four states. While the Populist Party eventually declined, many of its ideas were later adopted by the major parties, particularly the Progressive Movement.

Throughout the 20th century, the Progressive Party, also known as the Bull Moose Party, was led by former President Theodore Roosevelt. Several other third parties and independent candidates made notable contributions to American politics. The Socialist Party, led by figures such as Eugene V. Debs, consistently advocated for labor rights, social welfare programs, and an end to capitalism.

The Civil Rights Movement and anti-Vietnam War sentiment gave rise to new third-party efforts in the 1960s and 1970s. The American Independent Party, led by segregationist George Wallace, gained significant support in the 1968 presidential election, while the Peace and Freedom Party united anti-war activists, feminists, and civil rights advocates.

In recent years, independent candidates such as Ross Perot, Ralph Nader, Jill Stein, and Gary

Johnson have continued the tradition of third-party and independent challenges to the two-party system, bringing attention to issues such as government reform, environmental protection, and personal freedoms, and influencing the national political discourse even without winning major elections.

Past Successes And Failures

The history of third-party movements in the United States is marked by both successes and challenges. While they rarely win major elections, they often influence the political agenda and introduce new ideas. One notable success was the rise of the Republican Party in the 1850s, which emerged after the collapse of the Whig Party and the rise of the Free Soil Party. Focusing on slavery, the party attracted a coalition of anti-slavery activists, former

Whigs, and Free Soilers. In 1860, Republican candidate Abraham Lincoln won the presidency, demonstrating that third parties can become major political forces under the right circumstances.

The late 19th century Populist Party, despite not winning the presidency, achieved significant success by electing members to Congress and state legislatures, influencing major party policies, and advocating for reforms like direct senatorial elections (17th Amendment) and progressive income taxes (26th Amendment). Their ability to mobilize rural and working-class voters for economic reform demonstrated the potential of third parties to drive policy changes.

The Progressive Party of 1912, led by Theodore Roosevelt, significantly influenced the

Democratic and Republican parties, focusing on progressive issues like labor rights, women's suffrage, and corporate regulation. Despite not winning the presidency, Roosevelt's campaign influenced the adoption of progressive reforms in subsequent decades.

Third parties have faced numerous challenges, including the American electoral system's winner-take-all format and single-member district plurality voting system, which favors a two-party structure. Votes for third-party candidates are often seen as wasted, leading voters to choose the "lesser of two evils" among major parties.

Ballot access laws, which vary by state but often require large signatures or stringent requirements, also pose a significant challenge for third-party candidates. These laws consume time and resources that third parties often lack compared to established major parties, making it difficult for them to gain seats.

Third-party candidates face a significant challenge in terms of media coverage, as major parties dominate the media, making it difficult to gain visibility and reach a broad audience.

Financial resources are also a major hurdle, as political campaigns in the United States are expensive and major parties have strong fundraising networks. Third parties often struggle to compete financially, limiting their ability to run effective campaigns.

The perception that third-party candidates cannot win is a significant psychological barrier that discourages potential supporters from voting. To overcome this perception, successful campaigning and changes to the electoral system are required.

Third parties play a crucial role in American politics, bringing new ideas, influencing major party platforms, and addressing voter dissatisfaction. Their successes and failures provide valuable lessons for current and future third-party movements. Understanding these dynamics helps third parties navigate the political landscape and achieve their goals.

In summary,

Despite facing challenges and struggling to achieve major electoral victories, their impact on American politics is significant. They introduce important issues, influence major party platforms, and provide a voice for voters dissatisfied with the status quo. As the political landscape evolves, third parties remain an essential and dynamic component of American democracy, challenging the two-party system and advocating for alternative governance visions.

CHAPTER 2

The Current Political Climate

Voter Dissatisfaction With Major Parties

Voter dissatisfaction with the two major political parties in the United States, Democratic and Republican, has reached an unprecedented level. This discontent is driven by a complex interplay of factors, including economic inequality, political corruption,

rejoining the Paris Agreement and proposing the Green New Deal. However, critics argue that their efforts have been insufficient and often compromised by corporate interests. On the other hand, the Republican Party has largely resisted comprehensive climate action, with many members denying the scientific consensus on climate change or prioritizing economic concerns over environmental protection. This lack of decisive action has left many voters, particularly younger ones, feeling disillusioned.

Foreign policy is another area where voter dissatisfaction is evident. The long wars in Iraq and Afghanistan, coupled with ongoing military engagements around the world, have led to a growing wariness of further military interventions. Many Americans are skeptical of the country's foreign policy priorities and question the effectiveness of its international engagements. The major parties' handling of these issues has often been seen as disconnected from the realities and desires of the electorate.

The increasing polarization and partisanship in American politics have further exacerbated voter dissatisfaction. The major parties are often seen as more interested in scoring political points and vilifying their opponents than in governing effectively. This has led to a political stalemate where compromise is rare and legislative progress is often stymied. Many voters feel that the major parties are more focused on maintaining power than on addressing the pressing issues facing the nation.

The rise of populism has also played a role in voter dissatisfaction. Politically ignored people have fueled left- and right-wing populist movements. Figures like Bernie Sanders and Donald Trump have tapped into this sentiment, offering starkly different visions for the country but sharing a common theme of challenging the status quo. While these movements have energized certain segments of the electorate, they have also deepened divisions and highlighted the inadequacies of the major parties in addressing the concerns of many voters.

Corruption and ethics scandals have further undermined trust in the major parties. High-profile cases of corruption, insider trading, and misuse of office have tarnished the reputations of politicians from both parties. This perception of widespread corruption contributes to a sense of cynicism and disillusionment among voters, who feel that the political system is rigged in favor of the powerful and well-connected.

In addition to these substantive issues, there is a growing sense that the major parties are out of touch with the everyday lives of ordinary Americans. The political elite is often seen as living in a bubble, disconnected from the struggles and concerns of the average citizen. This perception is fueled by the increasing professionalization of politics, where many politicians come from privileged backgrounds and have little real-world experience outside of the political arena.

As a result of these various factors, there is a growing appetite for alternatives to the major parties. Many voters are seeking new voices and new ideas that can break the cycle of partisan gridlock and offer real solutions to the country's problems. This has created an opening for third-party and independent candidates who can present themselves as genuine alternatives to the status quo.

However, the path for these alternatives is fraught with challenges. The structural barriers to third-party success, including ballot access laws, the winner-take-all electoral system, and limited media coverage, make it difficult for these candidates to gain traction. Additionally, the perception that a vote for a third-party candidate is a wasted vote remains a significant hurdle.

Despite these obstacles, the growing dissatisfaction with the major parties suggests that there is significant potential for third-party movements to gain support. By addressing the concerns that the major parties have failed to resolve and offering a compelling vision for the future, third-party candidates can tap into the deep well of voter frustration and discontent. This book aims to explore these possibilities and provide a roadmap for those seeking to challenge the dominance of the major parties and create a more inclusive and responsive political system.

Increasing Polarization

The current political climate in America is distinguished by increased polarization, profound ideological divides, and extreme partisanship. This polarization has enormous ramifications for government, public debate, and the health of democracy; therefore, understanding its roots and repercussions is critical for future political developments. The ideological homogenization of the Democratic and Republican parties, with liberals aligning with the Democratic Party and conservatives with the Republican Party, has led to a stark contrast, shrinking the political middle ground and making compromise difficult.

The media's role in polarization is significant, with cable news networks and online outlets creating an "echo chamber" effect that reinforces partisan views and reduces the consumption of balanced, objective news. Social media platforms, designed to maximize engagement, further amplify this effect by promoting content that elicits strong emotional reactions, often at the expense of nuanced debate and reasoned arguments.

Gerrymandering, the practice of creating electoral districts for one party, has led to polarization. Politicians who create "safe" districts are less likely to appeal to the political center, resulting in more ideologically extreme representatives. This polarization in legislative bodies makes bipartisan cooperation more challenging. Therefore, it is crucial to address gerrymanding's effects on political outcomes.

Economic factors, such as rising inequality in the US, contribute to polarization among Americans, leading to feelings of insecurity and frustration. This discontent can fuel political extremism as individuals seek radical solutions. The economic divide often intersects with geographic and educational divides, with urban, educated populations leaning liberal and rural, less-educated populations leaning conservative, creating distinct cultural and political identities at odds.

Polarization in politics is exacerbated by the political strategies of major parties. Both parties have increasingly used negative campaigning, targeting their opponents rather than promoting their policies. This strategy mobilizes the base but deepens divisions and creates a toxic political environment. Fear and anger are used as mobilizing tools, making opponents seem like existential threats.

This polarization has led to legislative gridlock, making it nearly impossible to pass significant legislation. This gridlock is often seen during periods of divided government, where one party controls the presidency and the other controls Congress. Even when one party holds all three houses, internal divisions can still hinder progress, as seen in the difficulties faced by both parties.

Polarization in the judicial system has led to a highly contentious process for appointing judges, with both parties seeking to align with their ideological views. This has resulted in a polarized judiciary, with decisions often reflecting the judges' ideological leanings rather than impartial legal reasoning. Polarization also affects social relationships, with individuals segregating themselves based on political beliefs, leading to social fragmentation and the perception of disagreements as personal attacks, further deepening divisions.

Polarization undermines trust in democratic institutions by making individuals perceive the other side as wrong or illegitimate. This can lead to escalating distrust and conflict, with each side viewing the other as a threat to democracy. The 2020 presidential election and subsequent attacks on the Capitol highlighted the dangers of this erosion of trust.

Addressing polarization is a complex challenge, but efforts to promote electoral reforms, media literacy, and civic education programs can help reduce extreme partisanship. Encouraging diverse sources of information and promoting media literacy can also help mitigate the echo chamber effect and foster a more informed public discourse.

Promoting dialogue and understanding between individuals from different political backgrounds can help reduce polarization and build mutual respect. Programs like "Living Room

Conversations" and "Better Angels" create spaces for such dialogues, fostering a more cohesive society.

Reforming the political process to encourage moderate and representative candidates is also crucial. This includes reducing the influence of money in politics, such as through public campaign financing and stricter donation regulations. Open primaries or nonpartisan blanket primaries can ensure that extreme candidates do not dominate the electoral process.

Addressing economic inequality and providing economic security for all Americans can reduce polarization. Policies focusing on creating good-paying jobs, improving access to education and healthcare, and ensuring a fairer distribution of wealth can address grievances fueling political extremism. A more equitable society can diminish the appeal of radical and divisive politics.

Overcoming polarization requires commitment from political leaders and citizens to prioritize the health of the democratic system over short-term partisan gains. Political leaders must engage in good-faith negotiations and seek common ground, even taking unpopular positions within their own parties. Citizens must be open to listening to and understanding different perspectives, engage in civil discourse, and resist demonizing those with different opinions. Fostering a culture of respect and empathy can contribute to a more constructive and less polarized political environment.

In summary

The growing polarization in American politics poses significant challenges to governance, social cohesion, and democracy. To tackle this, a multifaceted approach is needed, including electoral reforms, media literacy and civic education initiatives, dialogue and understanding initiatives, and policies addressing economic inequality. By understanding and addressing polarization, political leaders and citizens can create a more inclusive and united political system.

CHAPTER 3

Challenges Facing Third Parties

Ballot Access Issues

Ballot access concerns are among the most significant challenges that third parties confront in the United States. These challenges originate from the numerous and frequently onerous rules that differ by state, making it impossible for third-party candidates to appear on ballots alongside their Democratic and Republican counterparts. High signature requirements, early filing deadlines, and hefty costs are all examples of ballot access restrictions aimed at benefiting established parties.

In many states, third-party candidates must collect a large number of signatures from registered voters in order to appear on the ballot. This signature collection procedure can be time-consuming and costly, necessitating large volunteer networks or hired petition circulators. For example, in places like California and Texas, the number of signatures required can be staggering, sometimes numbering in the tens of thousands. Furthermore, these signatures frequently need to be collected within a particular time frame, putting additional strain on third-party efforts.

The verification of these signatures can potentially be challenging. Election authorities may reject signatures for a variety of reasons, including minor errors in voter information or signatures that do not match voter registration records. This might result in a considerable amount of collected signatures being invalidated, forcing campaigns to collect more signatures than originally anticipated to meet requirements.The resources needed for this procedure may distract attention and funds away from more important campaign efforts, such as outreach and voter education.

Early filing deadlines are another challenge for third-party candidates. These deadlines are sometimes set months before the main election, requiring campaigns to mobilize rapidly and obtain the requisite signatures or fees well before the major parties announce their nominees. This early schedule may disadvantage third parties, who usually have fewer resources and organizational infrastructure than the big parties.

Filing expenses are also a significant obstacle. Some states require candidates to pay significant fees to get their names listed on the ballot. These fees can range from a few hundred to several thousand dollars, establishing a financial barrier that many third-party candidates find difficult to overcome. Major-party candidates frequently have established fundraising networks and party backing to cover these costs, but third-party candidates typically rely on smaller, grassroots donations.

In addition to these procedural hurdles, third parties frequently face legal challenges that seek to keep them off the ballot. Major parties or their supporters may file a lawsuit to challenge the legitimacy of third-party candidates' signatures or other components of their ballot access petition. These legal battles can be expensive and time-consuming, diverting resources away from already underfunded campaigns.

Moreover, the rules governing ballot access are often written and enforced by officials affiliated with the major parties, creating an inherent bias against third-party candidates. This can lead to inconsistent application of the rules and subjective decisions that further disadvantage third-party efforts. For example, election boards might be more lenient in interpreting signature requirements for major-party candidates while strictly scrutinizing third-party petitions.

The impact of these ballot access issues is profound. By making it difficult for third-party candidates to appear on the ballot, these barriers limit the choices available to voters and reinforce the dominance of the two major parties. This, in turn, perpetuates voter dissatisfaction with the political system and stifles the emergence of new ideas and perspectives that third parties often bring to the table.

Despite these challenges, there have been some efforts to reform ballot access laws and make the process more equitable. Advocacy groups and third-party organizations have pushed for changes such as reducing signature requirements, lowering filing fees, and standardizing the rules across states to create a more level playing field. Some states have made incremental progress in this area, but significant disparities and barriers remain.

Addressing ballot access issues is critical for reforming American democracy. Ensuring that all candidates, regardless of party affiliation, have a fair and reasonable opportunity to appear on the ballot can enhance voter choice, increase political competition, and encourage greater participation in the democratic process. It can also help to mitigate voter dissatisfaction by providing more diverse options and fostering a more inclusive and representative political system.

Debate Inclusion Barriers

In the United States, another significant challenge for third parties is gaining inclusion in the presidential and other major debates. These debates are crucial platforms for candidates to present their ideas to a wide audience and gain national visibility. However, third-party candidates often find themselves excluded from these debates due to stringent and often biased inclusion criteria set by debate organizers, particularly the Commission on Presidential Debates (CPD).

Since its inception in 1987, the CPD, a non-profit organization that sponsors and produces presidential and vice presidential debates in the United States, has served as the principal gatekeeper for debate inclusion. The CPD's guidelines for participation often include polling thresholds and other requirements that third-party candidates find difficult to achieve. To qualify for the debates, candidates must receive an average of 15% support in five national surveys, according to the CPD. This threshold is especially tough for third-party candidates, who frequently struggle to garner large polling numbers due to limited media coverage and the idea that voting for them is a waste of time.

Polling thresholds are problematic for several reasons. First, national polls often exclude third-party candidates from their questionnaires or present them as less viable options, skewing the results. Second, third-party candidates typically receive less media coverage, making it harder for them to reach the broader electorate and improve their poll numbers. The exclusion from debates thus becomes a self-fulfilling prophecy: without debate exposure, third-party candidates cannot improve their polling, and without sufficient polling, they cannot participate in debates.

Media bias also plays an important role in this exclusion. Major media outlets, which have a significant impact on public opinion and polling, frequently ignore third-party candidates in favor of focusing on Democratic and Republican candidates. This lack of coverage makes it difficult for third-party candidates to get the attention they require to increase their poll numbers and achieve debate inclusion standards. When third-party candidates do obtain media coverage, it is sometimes contemptuous or dubious, limiting their capacity to be regarded seriously by voters.

The consequences of being excluded from debates are profound. Debates provide candidates with a rare opportunity to speak directly to millions of voters, articulate their platforms, and confront their opponents. Exclusion from these platforms denies third-party candidates the opportunity to promote their ideas on an equal level with major-party candidates. It also fosters the notion that only the Democratic and Republican candidates are viable rivals, excluding other voices and opinions.

Efforts to reform debate inclusion criteria have faced significant resistance. Proposals to lower the polling thresholds, include more third-party candidates, or use alternative formats such as round-robin debates have been largely ignored by the CPD and other debate organizers. Legal challenges have also been unsuccessful, with courts often deferring to the CPD's discretion in setting its own rules.

Despite these challenges, there have been some notable instances where third-party candidates managed to participate in debates. The most famous example is the 1992 presidential election, where independent candidate Ross Perot was included in all three presidential debates. Perot's inclusion is widely credited with helping him secure 19% of the popular vote, the highest percentage for a third-party candidate in modern U.S. history. His participation demonstrated the potential impact of debate inclusion on third-party candidates and voter perceptions.

Another strategy for third-party candidates is to organize their own debates or seek alternative platforms to reach voters. For instance, some third-party candidates have participated in debates organized by media outlets, universities, or civic organizations that are more inclusive. While these debates typically do not attract the same level of national attention as the CPD-sponsored debates, they can still provide valuable exposure and opportunities to connect with voters.

Debate inclusion is crucial for a more competitive political landscape. Ensuring third-party candidates have a fair chance to participate in debates enhances voter choice, promotes diverse ideas, and encourages meaningful discourse. This can reduce dissatisfaction with major parties and strengthen the democratic process.

The Winner-Takes-All Electoral System

The winner-take-all electoral system, also known as first-past-the-post, presents a formidable challenge to third-party candidates in the United States. This system, used in most U.S. elections, including presidential, congressional, and many state and local elections, awards victory to the candidate who receives the most votes, regardless of whether they achieve an absolute majority. This structure inherently disadvantages third parties and reinforces the dominance of the two major parties.

The winner-takes-all system encourages strategic voting, leading to the "spoiler effect," where voters choose between two major party candidates they believe have a realistic chance of winning, even if neither fully represents their preferences. This discourages voters from supporting third-party candidates, whom they perceive as less likely to win and more likely to split the vote, potentially causing their least preferred major party candidate to win.

The spoiler effect was particularly noticeable in the 2000 presidential election, when Green Party candidate Ralph Nader's campaign was widely thought to have diverted votes from Democratic candidate Al Gore, resulting in the election of Republican candidate George W. Bush. This result reinforced the idea that voting for third-party candidates can have unforeseen and unfavorable implications, preventing people from supporting third-party campaigns in future elections.

Another consequence of the winner-takes-all system is the concentration of political power. Since only the candidate with the most votes wins, minority viewpoints and third-party platforms often go unrepresented, even if they have substantial support. This lack of representation leads to a political landscape dominated by the two major parties, which can become increasingly polarized and less responsive to the needs and concerns of a diverse electorate.

The system also contributes to the creation of "safe" districts, where one party has a significant and consistent advantage. In these districts, the major parties have little incentive to appeal to a broader range of voters or to moderate their positions, further entrenching polarization. Safe districts reduce the competitiveness of elections and limit the potential for third-party candidates to make significant inroads. Without the possibility of winning or even influencing the outcome, third-party efforts in these districts often seem futile.

The winner-takes-all system also affects the allocation of resources and campaign strategies. Major parties, aware of the structural advantages, concentrate their efforts and funding on swing states and competitive districts where they have a realistic chance of winning. Third-party candidates, lacking similar resources, struggle to gain traction in these strategically targeted areas, further marginalizing their campaigns.

In contrast to the winner-takes-all system, proportional representation systems, used in many other democracies, allocate seats based on the percentage of votes each party receives. This system allows for greater representation of minority viewpoints and smaller parties, encouraging a more diverse and inclusive political landscape. Proportional representation reduces the spoiler effect and allows voters to support third-party candidates without fear of wasting their vote.

Efforts to reform the winner-takes-all system in the United States have included proposals for alternative voting methods such as ranked-choice voting (RCV) and instant-runoff voting (IRV). RCV allows voters to rank candidates in order of preference, ensuring that votes for third-party candidates are not wasted. If no candidate wins an outright majority, the candidate with the fewest votes is eliminated, and their votes are redistributed based on voters' next preferences. This process continues until a candidate achieves a majority, mitigating the spoiler effect and encouraging more diverse candidate participation.

Several cities and states have adopted ranked-choice voting, with positive outcomes. For instance, in Maine, where RCV was implemented for state and federal elections, third-party and independent candidates have gained more visibility and voter support. RCV has also been used in local elections in cities like San Francisco and Minneapolis, demonstrating its feasibility and benefits.

Another potential reform is the adoption of multi-member districts, where several representatives are elected from a single district rather than just one. This system, often combined with proportional representation, or RCV, can ensure that a wider range of political views are represented in legislative bodies. Multi-member districts can help break the duopoly of the major parties, provide opportunities for third-party candidates to win seats, and influence policy.

Legal and constitutional barriers to electoral reform present significant challenges. The U.S. Constitution grants states the authority to determine their own electoral rules, and changes to the winner-take-all system would require widespread state-level reforms or constitutional amendments. Achieving such reforms requires substantial political will and public support, which can be difficult to muster in the face of entrenched interests and resistance from the major parties.

Public education and advocacy are crucial for promoting electoral reform. Voters need to understand the limitations of the winner-take-all system and the benefits of alternatives like ranked-choice voting and proportional representation. Advocacy groups, such as FairVote and Represent Us, work to raise awareness, build coalitions, and push for legislative changes at the state and local levels.

Despite the challenges, there is growing momentum for electoral reform. Increased voter dissatisfaction with the major parties and the current political system has sparked interest in alternatives that can provide more choice and representation. Grassroots movements and successful implementations of ranked-choice voting in various jurisdictions serve as models for broader adoption.

In summary,

The winner-take-all electoral system poses significant challenges to third-party candidates in the United States, reinforcing the dominance of the two major parties and limiting voter choice. Addressing these challenges through electoral reform, such as adopting ranked-choice voting and proportional representation, can create a more inclusive and competitive political landscape. By ensuring that all voices are heard and represented, these reforms can enhance the democratic process, reduce voter dissatisfaction, and encourage the emergence of new ideas and perspectives in American politics.

CHAPTER 4

Opportunities For Third Parties

Leveraging Media And Technology

Media and technology allow third parties to overcome some of their traditional limitations in modern politics. Third parties can expand their reach, create support, and engage voters in new and meaningful ways by using digital platforms, social media, and innovative communication tactics.

Media and technology allow third parties to bypass major news outlets and political institutions, which is a big benefit. Third-party candidates can reach voters on Twitter, Facebook, Instagram, and YouTube. These platforms let candidates communicate with supporters and organize grassroots campaigns without spending much money. Third-party politicians can get followers and build communities on social media.

Third-party candidates like Libertarian Gary Johnson and Green Party Jill Stein used social media extensively during the 2016 and 2020 presidential campaigns. By sharing films, live broadcasts, and messages on these sites, they might reach voters who may not have seen their efforts on traditional media. Third-party candidates may stay relevant and communicate with voters in real time by creating viral content, participating in online debates, and responding quickly to current events.

Social media, campaign websites, email newsletters, and mobile applications are essential to modern political campaigns. Well-designed websites serve as hubs for campaign information, policy positions, volunteer sign-ups, and contribution portals.

Email newsletters help candidates maintain regular communication with their supporters, delivering updates, calls to action, and personalized messages. Mobile apps can offer interactive features, such as push notifications for events, donation connections, and direct communication with campaign officials.

Crowdfunding platforms like Kickstarter, GoFundMe, and ActBlue have also transformed political financing, giving third-party candidates an alternative to traditional big-money contributors and PACs. By appealing directly to supporters for small-dollar contributions, third-party candidates can generate large amounts of cash to support their campaigns. This grassroots fundraising technique not only helps level the financial playing field but also generates a foundation of loyal supporters who feel personally involved in the campaign's success.

Moreover, digital advertising offers a cost-effective means for third-party candidates to reach specific groups. Platforms like Google Ads and Facebook Ads allow campaigns to target their messages to specific voter segments based on criteria such as age, location, interests, and political affiliations. This customized approach helps maximize the impact of a limited advertising budget and guarantees that campaign themes resonate with the desired audience.

Another possibility given by media and technology is the use of data analytics and voter modeling. Advanced data analysis can help third-party campaigns find potential supporters, assess voter behavior, and optimize campaign strategy. By integrating data from voter registration records, social media interactions, and prior election results, campaigns may construct detailed voter profiles and tailor their outreach efforts more efficiently. Data-driven techniques enable third-party candidates to focus their resources on swing voters and critical demographics, improving their chances of making a substantial effect.

Technology also permits creative political techniques, such as virtual town halls, online petitions, and digital organizing. Virtual town halls allow politicians to communicate with voters around the country, fielding questions and discussing policy proposals in an interactive way. Online petitions can rally supporters around certain causes, generating public pressure and media attention. Digital organizing tools enable volunteers to coordinate efforts, share information, and arrange events, building a sense of community and collective action.

In addition to these direct campaign applications, media and technology can amplify third-party voices through independent and alternative media outlets. Podcasts, blogs, and YouTube channels focused on politics and current events provide platforms for in-depth discussions and interviews with third-party candidates. These media outlets often attract audiences disillusioned with mainstream news coverage and open to alternative perspectives. By engaging with independent media, third-party candidates can reach voters who are actively seeking diverse viewpoints and policy solutions.

Despite the opportunities presented by media and technology, third-party candidates must navigate challenges such as algorithmic biases, misinformation, and digital security. Social media algorithms often prioritize content from established parties and candidates, making it harder for third-party messages to gain visibility.

Additionally, misinformation and fake news can spread rapidly online, potentially undermining third-party campaigns. Ensuring digital security is also critical, as cyberattacks and data breaches can disrupt campaign operations and erode voter trust.

In summary

Media and technology offer transformative

opportunities for third parties to enhance their visibility, engage with voters, and build robust campaigns. By effectively leveraging social media, digital tools, crowdfunding, data analytics, and alternative media, third-party candidates can overcome traditional barriers and create a significant impact on the political landscape. Embracing these opportunities requires creativity, adaptability, and a strategic approach to maximize their potential and reach a diverse electorate.

Key Issues For Differentiation

For third-party candidates to succeed in the extremely competitive political scenario of the United States, they must differentiate themselves by focusing on critical topics that resonate with voters and set them apart from the major parties. Identifying and promoting these causes can help third-party candidates establish a different voting base, create media attention, and build a compelling narrative that challenges the status quo.

One of the most effective tactics for distinction is to target issues that are underrepresented or badly addressed by the big parties. This method allows third-party candidates to tap into voter discontent and offer themselves as credible alternatives. For instance, environmental sustainability and climate change have often been at the forefront of the Green Party's policies. By promoting policies such as renewable energy development, climate crisis solutions, and conservation, Green Party candidates appeal to people who prioritize environmental issues and are dissatisfied with the major parties' solutions.

Similarly, the Libertarian Party has distinguished itself by campaigning for a smaller government, individual liberty, and free-market ideals. Key topics like limiting government regulation, defending privacy rights, and encouraging economic freedom appeal to voters who feel that the major parties have deviated from these objectives. By constantly promoting these topics, Libertarian candidates can attract people who prioritize personal and economic liberty.

Healthcare reform is another crucial issue where third-party candidates can differentiate themselves. While Democrats and Republicans frequently focus on incremental changes to the existing system, third-party candidates might offer bold, sweeping reforms. For example, lobbying for a single-payer healthcare system or universal basic income can catch the attention of voters who are unsatisfied with the current healthcare landscape and seek radical changes. By proposing thorough and innovative policy suggestions, third-party politicians can position themselves as leaders on topics that directly influence voters' lives.

Criminal justice reform is an increasingly important area where third parties can make major advances. Both major parties have been condemned for their handling of criminal justice policy, including mass incarceration, police brutality, and systematic racism. Third-party candidates might differentiate themselves by campaigning for comprehensive criminal justice reform, including ending the war on drugs, enacting restorative justice approaches, and addressing racial imbalances in the legal system. Third-party politicians who emphasize justice and equity may appeal to voters seeking significant change in this area.

Economic inequality and worker rights are also significant territory for third-party differences. As wealth disparity continues to expand, many voters are disillusioned with the major parties' ability to address economic issues successfully. Third-party candidates can push for policies such as raising the minimum wage, expanding workers' rights, and introducing progressive tax measures to combat inequality. By associating themselves with the interests of working-class and marginalized populations, third-party candidates can establish a strong, loyal voter base.

Electoral reform is another significant subject for differentiation. Voters who are disgruntled with the two-party system and demand a more representative democracy are inclined to support third-party candidates who call for changes such as ranked-choice voting, proportional representation, and campaign finance reform. By portraying themselves as champions of a better and more inclusive political system, third-party politicians might appeal to voters who feel alienated by the current electoral process.

Foreign policy is an area where third parties can offer alternative ideas that challenge the bipartisan consensus. For instance, the Peace and Freedom Party has long promoted non-interventionist principles and resistance to armed engagements. By calling for diplomatic solutions, decreasing military spending, and fostering international cooperation, third-party candidates can attract voters who are critical of the major parties' foreign policy policies.

Addressing systemic corruption and government accountability is another crucial issue for differentiation. Many voters perceive the major parties as being influenced by corporate interests and political elites. Third-party candidates can advocate for transparency, anti-corruption measures, and greater accountability in government. By highlighting their independence from special interests and commitment to ethical governance, third-party candidates can build trust and support among voters who seek integrity in politics.

In addition to focusing on specific issues, third-party candidates can differentiate themselves through their approach to politics and campaigning. Emphasizing grassroots involvement, participatory democracy, and community engagement can set third-party candidates apart from the top-down structures of the major parties. By involving supporters in decision-making processes and prioritizing local issues, third-party campaigns can create a sense of ownership and empowerment among their voter base.

Effective communication is also vital for differentiation. Third-party candidates must articulate their positions clearly and persuasively, using various media channels to reach diverse audiences. Developing a strong, consistent message that highlights their unique perspectives and solutions is essential for capturing voter attention and building a compelling narrative.

In conclusion, key differentiation issues are critical for third-party candidates seeking to make an impact in U.S. politics. By addressing underrepresented issues, proposing bold reforms, and emphasizing integrity and grassroots engagement, third-party candidates can attract voters who are dissatisfied with the major parties and seek genuine alternatives.

Focusing on these issues and effectively communicating their message can help third-party candidates build a distinct and influential presence in the political landscape.

Building Grassroots Movements

Building grassroots movements is a fundamental strategy for third-party candidates aiming to create a strong and sustainable political presence. Grassroots movements leverage the power of ordinary people to drive political change from the ground up, emphasizing community involvement, volunteerism, and local organizing. For third-party candidates, building a successful grassroots movement involves several key elements: engaging and mobilizing supporters, creating a strong local presence, utilizing effective communication strategies, and fostering a sense of community and collective action.

Building a grassroots movement involves engaging and mobilizing supporters who are disillusioned with major parties and are open to third-party ideas. This can be achieved through local events, neighborhood canvassing, and social media use. Listening to supporters' concerns, understanding their priorities, and presenting a viable alternative is crucial for successful outreach.

Volunteers power grassroots movements. Third-party campaigns should recruit and train dedicated volunteers. Volunteers can help with canvassing, phone banking, event planning, and social media. Volunteers need resources and assistance to stay motivated and effective.

A strong local presence is also important for grassroots initiatives. Third-party candidates should form local chapters, organize town hall meetings, and attend community events to develop community support. This local presence builds confidence and shows a commitment to addressing voters' problems. Local chapters can organize activities, share information, and build a supportive community.

Building and maintaining a grassroots movement requires effective communication. Third-party candidates must communicate their ideas for change in clear, convincing ways. Utilizing a range of communication platforms, including social media, email newsletters, podcasts, and community forums, allows candidates to reach a broad audience and keep supporters informed and involved. Storytelling may be a powerful strategy for connecting with voters on an emotional level and highlighting the real-world impact of the third-party platform.

Digital tools and technology play a crucial part in modern grassroots organizing. Social media sites like Facebook, Twitter, and Instagram allow third-party campaigns to reach large audiences quickly and cost-effectively. These tools offer real-time communication, enabling candidates to respond to current events, give updates, and mobilize supporters for action. Additionally, modern tools such as online petitions, fundraising platforms, and voter contact databases can boost the efficiency and reach of grassroots activities.

Building a sense of community and collaborative action is vital for the long-term success of a grassroots movement. Third-party candidates should establish opportunities for supporters to engage with each other, share their experiences, and work together towards common goals. This sense of community can be fostered through frequent meetings, social activities, and collaborative initiatives. Encourage supporters to take ownership of the movement and contribute their ideas and skills, which helps to establish a strong, dedicated base that is involved in the campaign's success.

Grassroots movements also benefit from forming coalitions and alliances with other organizations and advocacy groups. By partnering with groups that share similar goals and values, third-party campaigns can expand their reach, pool resources, and amplify their impact. Coalitions can help third-party candidates gain credibility, attract new supporters, and influence public policy on key issues. Building these alliances requires effective networking, communication, and a willingness to collaborate on common objectives.

Fundraising is a vital component of building and sustaining a grassroots movement. Third-party candidates frequently rely on small-dollar donations from individual supporters rather than huge contributions from wealthy donors or political action committees. Grassroots fundraising techniques might include internet donation drives, crowdfunding campaigns, and local fundraising events such as house parties, benefit concerts, and community meals. By focusing on transparency and accountability in their fundraising efforts, third-party candidates can create trust and demonstrate their commitment to ethical standards.

Grassroots movements thrive on visible action and concrete outcomes. Third-party candidates should focus on obtaining real successes, whether it's winning a municipal election, passing a ballot initiative, or influencing public policy on a specific topic. These victories help generate momentum, excite supporters, and attract media attention. Highlighting these achievements with excellent narrative and media coverage can further support the movement and demonstrate its potential for actual change.

In addition to immediate goals, grassroots movements should also focus on long-term strategies for growth and sustainability. This includes developing leadership within the movement, investing in training and education for volunteers, and creating structures that can adapt and evolve over time. Building a pipeline of future candidates and leaders ensures the continuity and resilience of the movement beyond a single election cycle.

In summary,

Third-party candidates can significantly impact the political landscape by building grassroots movements. This strategy involves engaging supporters, establishing a strong local presence, using effective communication, and fostering community and collective action. By demonstrating commitment to representing diverse interests and values, these candidates can build a sustainable base of support and drive significant political change from the ground up.

CHAPTER 5

Case Study

Recent Third-Party Campaigns

In recent years, several third-party campaigns have made notable impacts on the American political landscape. These campaigns, while often facing significant challenges, have demonstrated the potential for third-party candidates to influence public discourse, attract voter support, and, in some cases, achieve electoral success. Here, we explore some of the most significant recent third-party campaigns and the lessons they offer for future efforts.

2016 Presidential Campaigns

The 2016 presidential election was a landmark year for third-party candidates, with both the Libertarian Party and the Green Party gaining unprecedented visibility and support. The campaigns of Gary Johnson, the Libertarian candidate, and Jill Stein, the Green Party candidate, highlighted key issues and attracted voters dissatisfied with the major party nominees, Hillary Clinton and Donald Trump.

1. ***Gary Johnson***, a former governor of New Mexico, ran on a platform emphasizing individual liberties, small government, and free-market principles. His campaign garnered significant media attention, especially during the early stages of the election. Johnson's

libertarian stance on issues such as drug legalization, non-interventionist foreign policy, and reducing government regulation resonated with a substantial segment of the electorate. Despite challenges such as exclusion from the presidential debates and limited campaign funding, Johnson received over 4 million votes, representing 3.28% of the popular vote. This was the highest vote total for a Libertarian candidate in U.S. history, signaling a growing interest in third-party alternatives.

In Gary Johnson's campaign, "drug legalization" refers to the policy of making certain currently illegal drugs legal to use, possess, and sell under regulated conditions. This typically includes the legalization of marijuana for recreational and medicinal use, but may also extend to the decriminalization or legalization of other controlled substances. The goal behind this policy is to reduce the harms associated with drug prohibition, such as mass incarceration, and to allow adults to make their own choices regarding drug use. Additionally, it often includes implementing regulatory frameworks to ensure safety and quality control.

2. Jill Stein, running for the Green Party, focused her campaign on environmental sustainability, social justice, and economic equity. Stein's platform included ambitious proposals such as the Green New Deal, which aimed to transition the U.S. to 100% renewable energy by 2030, and policies to address income inequality and healthcare reform. Stein's campaign, while smaller in scale than Johnson's, still managed to capture significant attention, particularly among progressive voters disillusioned with the Democratic Party. Stein received over 1.4 million votes, or 1.07% of the popular vote, marking an important milestone for the Green Party.

The 2016 third-party campaigns underscored several critical points for future candidates. Firstly, they demonstrated the importance of clear, distinctive platforms that address underrepresented issues. Both Johnson and Stein attracted voters by focusing on policies that were either ignored or inadequately addressed by the major parties. Secondly, the campaigns highlighted the challenges of gaining media coverage and access to debates, which remain significant barriers for third-party candidates. Lastly, the 2016 election showed that even without winning, third-party candidates could influence public discourse and push major parties to address their issues.

2020 Presidential Campaigns

The 2020 presidential election saw continued efforts from third-party candidates, although the political landscape was dominated by the intense contest between Donald Trump and Joe

Biden. Despite this, the Libertarian Party and Green Party once again fielded candidates who aimed to provide alternatives to the major party nominees.

1. *Jo Jorgensen*, the Libertarian candidate, ran on a platform similar to Gary Johnson's, emphasizing personal freedom, non-interventionist foreign policy, and free-market economics. Jorgensen, a psychology professor and longtime Libertarian activist, focused on issues such as criminal justice reform, ending the war on drugs, and reducing government overreach. Her campaign faced significant hurdles, including limited media coverage and exclusion from the presidential debates. Nonetheless, Jorgensen received nearly 1.9 million votes, or 1.18% of the popular vote, demonstrating continued support for libertarian principles.

2. *Howie Hawkins*, the Green Party candidate, campaigned on an expanded version of the Green New Deal, advocating for comprehensive climate action, economic justice, and universal healthcare. Hawkins, a co-founder of the Green Party, aimed to build on Jill Stein's previous campaigns by addressing the interconnected crises of climate change, economic inequality, and healthcare. Hawkins' campaign, like Jorgensen's, struggled with limited media exposure and resources but succeeded in highlighting key progressive issues. Hawkins received over 400,000 votes, or 0.25% of the popular vote.

The 2020 third-party campaigns highlighted a number of ongoing challenges and opportunities for third-party candidates. The COVID-19 pandemic and heightened political polarization created an environment where third-party messages struggled to break through. However, the campaigns of Jorgensen and Hawkins demonstrated the importance of persistence and the need for innovative strategies to engage voters. Additionally, the 2020 election underscored the critical role of digital and social media in reaching and mobilizing supporters, especially when traditional media avenues are limited.

Lessons From Recent Campaigns

Several key lessons can be drawn from these recent third-party campaigns:

1. Clear and Distinctive Platforms: Successful third-party campaigns have distinct, clear platforms that address issues neglected by major parties. Candidates must offer compelling alternatives that resonate with voters' concerns and aspirations.

2. Grassroots Mobilization: Building a strong grassroots movement is crucial. Engaging volunteers, creating local chapters, and fostering community involvement can amplify the campaign's reach and impact.

3. Innovative Communication: Leveraging digital tools and social media is essential for reaching a broad audience. Third-party candidates must use these platforms to engage with voters, share their messages, and mobilize support.

4. Persistence and adaptability: Third-party campaigns face numerous obstacles, including media bias and exclusion from debates. Persistence and the ability to adapt strategies in response to challenges are vital for sustaining momentum.

5. Building Alliances: Forming coalitions with advocacy groups and other organizations can expand the campaign's reach and influence. Partnerships can help third-party candidates gain credibility and support.

6. Focus on Electoral Reform: Advocating for electoral reforms, such as ranked-choice voting and proportional representation, can help third-party candidates challenge the structural advantages of the major parties and create a more level playing field.

In summary,

Recent third-party campaigns in the United States have demonstrated both the potential and challenges for third-party candidates. By learning from these experiences and continuing to innovate, third-party candidates can build on their successes and work towards creating a more diverse and representative political landscape.

Profiles Of Current Candidates (2024)

The 2024 election cycle is witnessing the rise of several third-party candidates from diverse backgrounds, aiming to challenge the dominance of the two major parties and advocate for policies that cater to the needs and concerns of a broader electorate. *These candidates, presenting a range of ideologies, are profiled, and their platforms include:*

1. Libertarian Party: Chase Russell Oliver

Chase Russell Oliver is the Libertarian Party's presidential nominee for 2024, his nomination was announced on 12th of April 2024. He is running with Mike ter Maat as his vice presidential candidate. Mike ter Maat, who has a background in economics and law enforcement, brings a complementary perspective to the ticket. Chase is known for his strong advocacy of individual liberties, limited government, and free markets, Oliver's platform focuses on issues such as criminal justice reform, ending the war on drugs, and reducing government interference in the economy.

Oliver's background as an activist and political organizer has equipped him with the skills to engage and mobilize voters effectively. He emphasizes personal freedom, advocating for policies that protect civil liberties and reduce the government's role in individuals' lives. His commitment to libertarian principles and ability to connect with voters through grassroots efforts make him a key figure in the Libertarian Party's bid for greater political influence.

2. Green Party: Jill Ellen Stein

Jill Stein, the Green Party's presidential candidate in 2012 and 2016, is once again leading the party in 2024. Her vice presidential running mate is Ajamu Baraka. Stein and Baraka previously ran together in the 2016 election and have a platform focused on addressing climate change, economic inequality, and promoting an "economic bill of rights" for all Americans, which includes guaranteed employment, healthcare, housing, food, and education. Stein is a longtime activist and advocate for environmental sustainability, social justice, and economic equity. Her platform focuses on the Green New Deal, which aims to address climate change through comprehensive economic and environmental reforms. Her advocacy for universal healthcare, student debt cancellation, and a living wage resonates with progressive voters who seek bold, transformative policies.

Stein's background as a physician and environmental health advocate provides her with a strong foundation to address public health and environmental issues. Her commitment to grassroots organizing and community engagement makes her a compelling candidate for voters who feel marginalized by the major parties. Stein's emphasis on intersectional approaches to policy and her dedication to building inclusive movements have made her a prominent figure within the Green Party

3. Robert F. Kennedy Jr., an independent runner

In the 2024 election, Robert F. Kennedy Jr. is vying for the presidency as an independent candidate. Initially launching his campaign as a Democrat, Kennedy later chose to pursue an independent bid, officially declaring his candidacy on October 9, 2023, in Philadelphia. Kennedy's platform focuses on a range of issues, including economic policies aimed at restoring the middle class, advocating for higher wages, affordable housing, and reducing military spending to fund domestic programs.

Kennedy's campaign emphasizes individual liberties, transparency in government, and anti-corruption measures. He proposes to raise the minimum wage, prosecute union-busting corporations, expand free childcare, lower housing costs, cut energy prices, support small businesses, secure the border, and negotiate fair trade deals. He also advocates for reining in military spending to reallocate funds towards infrastructure, healthcare, education, and other domestic needs.

Kennedy's running mate is Nicole Shanahan, a tech entrepreneur, who complements his campaign with her focus on innovation and technological advancements. Together, they aim to present a viable alternative to the major parties by addressing the pressing issues faced by many Americans and promoting a vision of economic and social justice.

In summary

The 2024 election cycle offers a chance for third-party and independent candidates to have a big impact on the American political landscape. These candidates are striving to transcend traditional hurdles and present realistic alternatives to the electorate by providing unique platforms, engaging in grassroots organizations, and harnessing digital media. As voter dissatisfaction with the major parties grows, the efforts of third-party and independent candidates could have a significant impact on the future of American politics.

CHAPTER 6

Strategies For Success

Third-party and independent candidates have distinct hurdles in the highly competitive and frequently harsh political environment in the United States. However, with strategic planning and excellent execution, they may create long-term movements, engage and retain voters, and produce compelling policy views that appeal to them. The following are strategies for success in these important areas:

Building A Sustainable Movement

1. Grassroots organizing: Grassroots organization is crucial for any third-party movement. It entails mobilizing volunteers and supporters at the local level to engage with the community, convey the party's message, and develop a stable base of support. This can be achieved through door-to-door canvassing, community events, and local chapters. Grassroots activities can build a sense of ownership and commitment among supporters, which is vital for long-term sustainability.

2. Establishing a clear vision and mission: A clear and appealing vision is vital for developing a sustainable movement. This involves identifying the party's core principles, aims, and long-term ambitions. The vision should be presented consistently and effectively across all platforms to ensure that supporters understand and buy into the movement's objective. For example, the Green Party's emphasis on environmental sustainability and social justice provides a distinct and uniting topic for its followers.

3. Building strong leadership and governance structures: Effective leadership and effective governance mechanisms are important for maintaining a political movement. This includes having a clear organizational hierarchy, transparent decision-making processes, and methods for accountability. Strong leadership creates confidence and trust among followers, while solid governance ensures that the movement can run efficiently and respond to crises effectively.

4. Securing funding and resources:B Financial stability is vital for any political organization.

Third-party candidates often experience difficulty in fundraising compared to their main party counterparts. Therefore, they need to implement new fundraising tactics, such as small-dollar gifts, crowdsourcing campaigns, and leveraging social media channels to contact potential contributors. Building a network of loyal contributors who contribute consistently can provide a steady stream of resources needed for campaign operations.

5. Forming alliances and coalitions: Forming connections with like-minded organizations and advocacy groups can increase a third party's impact. These coalitions can give more resources, enhance the party's reach, and increase its impact on crucial issues. For instance, the Libertarian Party has regularly partnered with civil liberties organizations to achieve its platform on decreasing government intrusion and safeguarding individual freedoms.

6. Developing a long-term strategy: Building a viable movement demands a long-term plan that goes beyond specific electoral cycles. This involves creating incremental goals, identifying critical milestones, and developing plans for growth and expansion. A long-term vision permits the movement to generate momentum over time and adapt to shifting political conditions.

Engaging And Retaining Voters

1. Effective communication and messaging: Clear and consistent messaging is crucial for engaging and retaining voters. Third-party candidates must communicate their viewpoints on crucial issues in a way that resonates with the voters. This means employing plain, relevant language and addressing the needs of regular citizens. Tailoring communications to different demographic groups can also boost engagement. For example, focusing on economic measures that benefit working-class families can attract voters who feel abandoned by the big parties.

2. Leveraging digital media and technology: In the digital age, leveraging social media and technology is vital for reaching and engaging voters. Platforms like Twitter, Facebook, and Instagram allow candidates to communicate directly with supporters, convey their thoughts, and motivate action. Additionally, using data analytics to understand voter preferences and habits might help in developing focused campaigns that address specific problems and objectives of the public.

3. Hosting town halls and public forums: Town halls and public forums give opportunities for direct engagement between candidates and citizens. These gatherings allow candidates to address issues, clarify their viewpoints, and create personal connections through attendance. Engaging with voters in person helps establish trust and indicates a candidate's commitment to listening to and representing the people.

4. Building a strong volunteer network: Volunteers are the backbone of any political campaign. Building a strong network of dedicated volunteers who are passionate about the party's mission can dramatically increase voter engagement efforts. Volunteers can assist with canvassing, phone banking, event organization, and voter outreach, generating a widespread and personal touch that can resonate with voters.

5. Voter education and empowerment: Educating voters about the electoral process and the importance of their participation can boost engagement. Providing information on how to register to vote, polling station location, and voting process can empower citizens to exercise their rights. Additionally, educating voters about the specific issues and policies the party advocates for can help them make informed decisions.

6. Maintaining continuous engagement: Engagement should not be limited to election seasons. Maintaining continuous engagement with voters through regular updates, newsletters, and community events helps keep the party and its issues at the forefront of voters' minds. Continuous engagement also helps to build a loyal base of supporters who are more likely to stay committed to the party in the long run.

Developing Compelling Policy Positions

1. Conducting comprehensive research: Developing convincing policy positions demands a solid understanding of the issues at hand. Conducting detailed research, engaging experts, and analyzing data are crucial elements in establishing well-informed policies. This guarantees that the party's positions are credible, realistic, and address the real demands of the electorate.

2. Focusing on key issues: Focusing on a few core themes that resonate most with people might boost a party's appeal. Identifying and prioritizing key topics based on voter concerns, such as healthcare, education, economic injustice, or climate change, allows the party to craft clear and impactful policy solutions. For example, the Green Party's focus on environmental sustainability and social justice addresses the basic issues of its target voter base.

3. Providing innovative solutions: Third-party candidates might differentiate themselves by presenting new and forward-thinking solutions to urgent challenges. This entails thinking outside the box and suggesting strategies that target underlying issues rather than just symptoms. For instance, Andrew Yang's proposal for a universal basic income during his 2020 campaign was a fresh notion that attracted substantial attention and support.

4. Ensuring Policy Coherence and Consistency: Consistency and coherence in policy positions are vital for creating credibility. Policies should fit with the party's core beliefs and long-term vision. Inconsistent or contradictory positions can destroy confidence and mislead voters. Clear and consistent messaging surrounding policy proposals supports the party's commitment to its ideals and aims.

5. Engaging stakeholders and communities: Involving stakeholders and communities in the policy formulation process can boost the relevance and acceptance of recommendations. This includes interacting with advocacy groups, community leaders, and affected communities to gather input and feedback. Collaborative policy creation ensures that the party's positions are inclusive and serve the demands of varied constituents.

6. Communicating Policy Benefits: Effectively conveying the benefits of proposed policies is vital for garnering voter support. This involves breaking down difficult topics into understandable words and showcasing the beneficial impacts on individuals and communities. Using real-life examples and tales can make policy ideas more relevant and persuasive to voters.

In summary

Third-party and independent candidates can achieve success by building sustainable movements, engaging and retaining voters, and developing compelling policy positions. These strategies require dedication, innovation, and a deep understanding of the political landscape and voter concerns. By addressing these areas effectively, third-party candidates can present themselves as viable alternatives to the major parties and make a significant impact on the political scene.

Conclusion

Future Outlook For Third-party Politics

The future of third-party politics in the United States has enormous promise, despite the considerable hurdles that these parties face. Growing dissatisfaction with the two major parties, increased political polarization, and the yearning for alternative answers to pressing challenges are creating a fertile field for third-party growth and influence.

The developing political scene is one significant component that will impact the future perspective. Voter unhappiness with the major parties is reaching record levels, driven by causes such as economic inequality, systematic corruption, and inadequate answers to climate change and healthcare crises. This frustration is forcing more people to investigate options beyond the traditional two-party system. For instance, a Gallup poll from early 2023 found that 62% of Americans felt a third major party was needed, showing a strong base of possible support for third-party candidates.

Technological advancements and the rise of social media are also significant. These platforms enable third-party candidates to reach and engage with voters more effectively and at a lesser cost than traditional media outlets. Social media channels, in particular, allow for direct engagement with the people, bypassing conventional media gatekeepers, who typically ignore third-party perspectives. This democratization of political communication can help level the playing field and offer third-party candidates a better chance to compete.

Furthermore, demographic trends are contributing to the potential for third parties to emerge. Younger generations, notably Millennials and Generation Z, tend to be more receptive to varied political ideas and are less likely to stick firmly to conventional party allegiance. These generations prioritize problems like climate change, social justice, and economic reform—areas where third-party candidates generally provide more inventive and radical ideas compared to the big parties.

However, considerable difficulties remain. The established two-party system, bolstered by electoral norms like the winner-takes-all mechanism and rigorous ballot access criteria, continues to offer serious obstacles. Overcoming these barriers will require ongoing efforts and strategic relationships. For example, third parties might profit from adopting electoral changes such as ranked-choice voting, which allows voters to rank candidates by preference and can help lessen the spoiler effect. Successful implementation of such measures in locations like Maine and New York City offers a template for widespread acceptance.

In the near future, we may anticipate third-party movements increasing their focus on creating coalitions, expanding their grassroots organizing efforts, and harnessing digital platforms to communicate with voters. As political polarization intensifies and the major parties fail to address the intricacies of contemporary challenges, the attractiveness of third-party candidates offering fresh viewpoints and answers is expected to expand.

In summary,

While the road ahead is laden with problems, the potential for third-party politics to transform the American political scene is substantial. With strategic preparation, excellent communication, and a focus on issues that resonate with a more diverse and unhappy audience, third parties can carve out a more substantial position in future elections.

Call To Action For Readers

As we conclude this exploration of third-party politics in the United States, it is crucial to recognize the power and responsibility that each of us holds as voters and citizens. The challenges facing third-party candidates are substantial, but so too are the opportunities for meaningful change.

Here's how you can contribute to this movement and make a difference:

1. Stay informed and educate others: Understanding the issues and policies proposed by third-party candidates is the first step toward making informed decisions. Take the time to research and learn about the platforms of various third-party candidates, and then share that knowledge with others. Use social media, community meetings, and other platforms to spread awareness and counteract misinformation.

2. Get involved in local politics: Local elections and grassroots movements are the backbone of any political change. Participate in your local community by attending town hall meetings, joining political clubs, or volunteering for third-party campaigns. Local involvement can lay the foundation for a broader national impact.

3. Support electoral reform: Advocate for electoral reforms that level the playing field for third-party candidates. Ranked-choice voting, proportional representation, and improved ballot access are essential innovations that can enable third parties to compete more effectively. Join organizations advocating for these reforms and contribute your voice to the cause.

4. Volunteer and donate: Campaigns, particularly those of third-party candidates, rely heavily on volunteers and small-dollar donations. Contribute your time, skills, or financial resources to help third-party candidates establish their campaigns. Whether it's phone banking, canvassing, or delivering professional services, every bit helps.

5. Vote consciously: Your vote is your voice; don't succumb to the misconception that voting for a third-party candidate is a wasted vote. If the candidate represents your beliefs and ideas better than the main parties, your vote for them is an essential declaration of your convictions. Encourage others to vote with their consciences, too.

6. Engage in civil discourse: Foster a culture of respectful and informed debate. Engage friends, family, and colleagues in discussions about third-party politics and the broader political system. Listening and understanding different perspectives can build bridges and foster a more inclusive political environment.

7. Hold elected officials accountable: Regardless of which party they belong to, hold your elected officials accountable for their actions and policies. Demand transparency, integrity, and responsiveness to the needs of the community. When officials know that voters are paying attention and willing to take action, they are more likely to act in the public interest.

In summary,

The path to a more vibrant and representative democracy requires active participation and engagement from all of us. Third-party politics offers a valuable avenue for addressing the shortcomings of the current system and bringing new ideas to the forefront. By staying informed, getting involved, supporting reforms, and voting with intention, we can help create a political landscape that truly reflects the diversity and aspirations of the American people. Your actions can make a difference starting today and be part of the movement for change.

Glossary Of Election Terms

1. Ballot Access: The requirements and rules that candidates must meet to appear on voters' ballots. This often includes collecting a certain number of signatures or paying a fee.

2. Campaign: An organized effort by a candidate or political party to win an election, which includes various activities such as speeches, advertisements, and rallies.

3. Electoral Reform: Changes proposed or enacted to improve the fairness, efficiency, or accessibility of the electoral system. Examples include ranked-choice voting and proportional representation.

4. Grassroots Movements: These are local or community-based movements that start from the bottom up, typically involving ordinary people working together to effect change.

5. Libertarian Party: A political party in the United States that emphasizes individual liberty, free markets, and limited government intervention.

6. Major Parties: The two dominant political parties in the U.S., namely the Democratic Party and the Republican Party,.

7. Non-Interventionist Foreign Policy: A policy stance advocating for minimal involvement in international conflicts and focusing on domestic issues instead.

8. Platform: The set of policies and positions that a candidate or political party supports and promotes during a campaign.

9. Polarization: the increasing division of political attitudes to ideological extremes, often resulting in a lack of common ground between opposing parties or viewpoints.

10. Presidential Debate: A formal discussion between presidential candidates in which they present their views on various issues, allowing voters to compare their positions.

11. Primary Election: An election held to determine which candidate will represent a political party in the general election.

12. Ranked-Choice Voting: An electoral system where voters rank candidates by preference rather than choosing just one, potentially reducing the spoiler effect and leading to more representative outcomes.

13. Spoiler Effect: When a third-party candidate takes votes away from a major-party candidate, potentially changing the outcome of the election.

14. Third Party: Any political party in the United States other than the two major parties (Democratic and Republican), such as the Libertarian Party or the Green Party.

15. Two-Party System: A political system dominated by two major parties, often presenting challenges for third-party candidates to gain traction and influence.

16. Vice-Presidential Candidate: The running mate of a presidential candidate who is nominated to serve as the Vice President if their ticket wins the election.

17. Ballot: The paper or electronic form used by voters to cast their votes in an election.

18. Electoral System: The method by which votes are counted and seats are allocated in an election. In the United States, this typically refers to the winner-takes-all system used in most elections.

19. Electorate: These are people in a country or area who are entitled to vote in an election.

20. Election: A general election is held to choose among candidates nominated in a primary for federal, state, or local office.

21. Libertarianism: This is a political philosophy that advocates for minimal state intervention in the personal and economic lives of individuals.

22. Nominee: The candidate selected by a political party to run for a particular office in an election.

23. Political Climate: The overall mood, attitudes, and opinions of the electorate and political environment at a given time.

24. Primary Campaign: The period during which candidates compete for their party's nomination before the general election.

25. Proportional Representation: This refers to an electoral system in which parties gain seats in proportion to the number of votes cast for them.

26. Ranked-Choice Voting: An electoral system in which voters rank candidates by preference, which can reduce the spoiler effect and lead to more representative outcomes.

27. Spoiler: A candidate whose presence in the election is perceived to draw votes from a major candidate, potentially affecting the outcome.

28. Swing State: A state in which no single candidate or party has overwhelming support, making it a key target for candidates in an election.

29. Third-Party Candidate: A candidate who runs for office representing a political party other than the two major parties.

30. Voter Turnout: This is the percentage of eligible voters who cast a ballot in an election.

31. Winner-Takes-All: An electoral system in which the candidate with the most votes wins and all other votes are not represented in the final outcome.

32. Youth Vote: This segment of the electorate is young voters, typically aged 18–29.

These terms help provide a comprehensive understanding of the concepts used in this book.

www.ingramcontent.com/pod-product-compliance
Lightning Source LLC
Chambersburg PA
CBHW061653250726
48659CB00004B/1482